MEANS TO AN END

Cover art by Donna Ong

Published by Landmark Books Pte Ltd
5001, Beach Road
#02-73/74
Singapore 199588

ISBN981-4189-18-9

Landmark Books is an imprint of Landmark Books Pte Ltd

Printed by Oxford Graphic Printers Pte Ltd

MEANS TO AN END

Toh Hsien Min

·LANDM△RK·BOOKS·

If the feeling of love is suppressed constantly, it hides in subconsciousness and exists there like a revolutionary going underground, plotting maliciously against consciousness and intending to blow it up. Contrary to this, Toh Hsien Min allows his feeling of love toward everything "we can remember" – and, above all, to the distant and nigh space – come out in the form of excellent poems. He is a poet-cartographer. Just as in his previous book *The Enclosure of Love*, Toh Hsien Min continues to keep a lyric diary of sorts, in which he records scrupulously the landscapes of the world and of his own soul.

- Regina Derieva, Russia.

The lyrical voice implicit in the narrative poetry of Toh Hsien Min is that of the modern city state's Everyman. The familiar and estranged go hand in hand with what is merely seemingly insignificant in this series of finely tuned philosophical observations, while gently mapping out the "emotional geographies" of modern life on each page. Reminiscent sometimes of Philip Levine or Billy Collins, Toh Hsien Min's new collection of poetry brings yet another proof to what is already certain: the continually strong stand of contemporary Singaporean poetry.

- Henrik C. Enbohm, Sweden

Whether he speaks about peeling a clementine, talking with God or not breaking a mirror, Toh Hsien Min is always waiting for you where you don't expect him to show up, a bunch of improbable flowers in his hand. His words are a genuine mixture of observation, reflection and humour, opening up onto challenging insights.

- Jacques Rancourt, Canada/France

For Arthur Yap

(1943 – 2006)

CONTENTS

THE BRIDGES

I cannot remember where it was, with the bridges,
Manchester City on the telly and me wanting
to watch the game in a black-beamed Irish pub.
Was it Toledo, which means that I was in love
with you? Or was it Austria, or Amsterdam,
in which case I was fuming at someone
whom in time to come I would see as benign?
I seem to recall three bridges, two lit, going
in different directions, one under reconstruction.
It could have been anywhere with three bridges.
The only reason that I remember is that
you were, or she was, with me. All this conflation,
that you should even be thought of
in the same instant as an erstwhile adversary,
confirms what others might find easier to deny.
If nothing else should come to recollect these
scattered fragments of less-than-Fujichrome,
I imagine I would learn, and keep in heart, that
my mind has been bounded by more than it
possibly can have taken in, and the touch
of a spiralling leaf in a boulevard can exert
more concrete influence in less tactility than
we can imagine, for we imagine we want to
remember more than we can remember, or want to.

SLOPE

And then there was the slope,
a flannel-fuzz of young green,
sun-soaked, wind-threshed,
and damp-earth-scented.
If it was tingling with couples
lounging on picnic mats,
charged with ultimate frisbee
and streaked by a golden retriever
bounding from teenage girl to dad,
and if up the road the chimes
of an ice-cream van, side-panel
hooked perpendicular for shade,
called out to all summer's people,
and if the bitumen gave way again
to the wearing of a pale clay track
leading to a scattering of firs,
it tremored like the surface circles
whenever a yellowed leaf quavers
onto a forest pool of my mind,
and I tried to remember where it was
this could be that had returned
with the authority of dream,
and as little access. Other paths
were only chains of elsewhere
that did not promise to lead
where the hand strokes water
as a favourite cat. For days that
couldn't seem to find their way out
I kept a slipping hold until
tonight I trace a path I had known
and startle myself when I do get it:
the rectangular porch of the hostel,
late afternoon in Leith, where
I spent a night because the Heart

was full; and just as soon again
I find myself disbelieving,
merging it into another slope
in Antrim or on Pacific Highway One,
as though identity murders mystery,
disqualifies the slope from its place
in dream, that never presence
that is ever absence, more real
than catalogued memory,
less unforgiving than clarity,
although the slope, once found,
will never be that one sheep
lost in the ravine, by a forest pool.

BIRTH OF THE MODERN CITY-STATE

Now that we are here, now that to the left you see
the stage-managing, perspectivally mobile chrysalides
and the pier making the newly perched Merlion
photographable from the sea, we must remember to turn
right to the Cenotaph and the Tan Kim Seng Fountain.

When we drink water we should remember the source.

I remember squatting on the airport runway in Kuala Lumpur,
taking a leak. Never had such a puddle seemed such abundance,
on the presumably hot tarmac. I don't remember the plane.
I remember leaning out of the window of the KTM train
on the way up. I remember a cake in the shape of a ship.
I was two. A candle danced flamenco on each iced funnel.
I remember our pomeranian, Hua Lang. Her beautiful russet coat.
One day I woke to news that she was gone. I never really found out
what happened. I think I assumed she ran away, but she could have
been knocked down by an insouciant car, or even given away
because we were due to move to an HDB flat in Tanglin Halt.
I don't recall if this was as close to when we moved as that.
Waiting for my parents to dress for dinner, when I was five,
I tried to figure out the difference between "has" and "have",
or "has" and "had". I remember my dad's Austin. It was
fire-engine red. I sat at the wheel, pretended to drive. Wondered how
anybody could see where he was going, the windscreen was so high.
I feigned sleep when the car drew into the parking lot, so dad
had to carry me all the chest-warm way to bed. I was a fat baby,
but a thin boy. I remember scraping the soles of my feet
on the yellow tiles of Yan Kit Pool, gulping water more often than
swimming, eventually giving up and peeking into the skanky drains
along the sides. I remember being badly seasick in a rocking boat
a mile from Tioman, clutching a line wound around a soda can
and desperately hoping the horizon would still. Back on shore
I clambered about the rocks with a fishing net, looking for fry.

My mother got stuck in a depth of thick black mud. Lost her shoe.

I remember all that now because of who I am, or the other way around.
I could have remembered sticking my head out the car while it jolted
through the oil-palm plantations of Johore. I could have remembered
photographing a barbecue pit by only half-accidentally pressing
the grey button. I could have remembered picking up a dollar note
on the double yellow lines beside the gate, light aluminium painted silver,
at my first home in MacPherson.

And the lines that run from the flared-sun present, here,
on a Wilkie Road sidewalk, to that far and fantastical land,
the past, run with the clearly fading presence of increasing distance.
We are here because we only remember. We only remember because
there was something in each of these streetlamps of memory
to fix them beside those double yellow lines. There was
only something because of the architecture of the city
to which we all subscribe, and which still shapes and
outlines what we are for as long as we are it.

HOME IMPROVEMENT

Sunday is the day in my estate for home improvement,
for it seems that every man in every household
rolls up his sleeves and gets the paint-rollers and step-ladders
and paints the wall that a dark patterned fungus has adopted
or fixes the fluorescent light in the balcony that doesn't work
or puts up rattan blinds to filter out the light of the tropical sun.
I'm not one to fix anything that hasn't been broken
twice over, but two weekends into the replacement home
I've asked in a contractor recommended by the *jaga*.
It does seem a little odd to me, like a gaping-hulled boat
beached in a desert, the water snatched from beneath its keel,
to be moaning that my old home, with its high ceilings,
interior space and spiral staircases, would be torn down,
and mere months later to be irked enough that a glass pane
on the 1960s folding doors had a crack like the break of tides at dawn
as to be countenancing their removal for aluminium sliding doors.
Maybe love is tempered by the cruelty of previous loss.
Once you have truly loved one it's hard to love another.
Or maybe, if you can hold two convictions of opposing force
in the one mind, this is my revenge, the wrath of bitter age,
my symbol of resistance to all those who would change things.
I would change enough to change things. If it is true that loss
is entirely contained within change and memory is the assertion
of that loss, then we can only remember by applying new force
to the other, precipitating wreckage to high-water-mark the sand.

WORTH REMEMBERING

When we were painting the living
room we spread newspapers
on the floor, to protect the old
ceramic tiles. They were from
the Sixties or Seventies, hence fast
dying out in a city that did not
want to remember its past, unless
it could make money out of it,
usually by sexing up the myth.
To appropriate a *Straits Times*
thus was both improper and quite
unremarkable, except that I
started reading old news: how
Bill O'Reilly had said on his show
that if Saddam had no WMDs, he
would apologise to the nation and
never trust the Bush administration
again, or what Ralph Reed supposed
to be a sign of success, not failure.
Well, my housemate was after me
because of my failure to get more
than a third of the way through
the anterior wall, and if I let sections
of wall dry before I returned to
smoothen them out I would have
unsightly patches, so could I
please get on with it, she really
should have borrowed someone
else's *Lianhe Zaobao*, in which case
I would probably have only looked
at photos. If in George W.'s world
being President meant he didn't
have to explain, then surely some
of these privileges should extend

to us who had looked to him for an
example, of some sort at any rate.
And if in that process, while pouring
Mayan yellow out like cream and
dipping my roller into it, I relearned
memory like a clot of paint soaking
and hardening old newsprint into
something less easily disposed of,
I don't dare say that anyone was any
better off for it; but that we had
a new coat of responsive yellow
for the afternoons of warm clarity
pouring in from the monsoonless
skies – that was worth remembering.

WHAT WORK FULFILS

Imagine that you were a Trappist monk.
Your order sought to separate from secular society,
and to revive the austerity of the early Cistercians
and their convictions on the rule of St Benedict.
Over the years you labour in the fields, raising horses,
cattle, hogs, sheep and chickens, sowing barley,
wheat, oats and corn, planting potatoes and carrots,
grinding grain into a fine dust in the old but functional
hand mills. You work the butter churn and the rennet.
For under the rule of St Benedict, you must live on
the work you create. If there is a participation
in the creative fuse of your God, you see it
coalescing with the curds, smell it wafted from
the oven where your bread is pregnant with yeast,
and feel it in the refreshed ache in your biceps,
from turning the churn, sixty times a minute.
In this way your products gladden your heart,
when you partake of the bread and the liquid bread
also. From mattins through to evening prayer,
you sanctify the land by what you gently
skim from it.
        You are an office worker however.
Trapped in a six-by-six cubicle forty floors up
in prime Grade 'A' Republic Plaza, where
you send invisible packets through an invisible
gateway into invisible networks to
invisible functionaries, you cannot help but
glaze over the windows at the view once dotted
with semi-cylindrical sampans, now shiny,
like sheet metal, with a sun you do not feel.
You sit in meetings where your boss tells you off
in front of your clients, prepare papers that will be
marked with red ink like your seven-year-old's
exercise book, pick up the phone to lie to people

who could just as wearily decide to commit
a sum that comes to one basis point of the budget
for that financial year to your stewardship, even if it is
eight times as large as what appears on the coloured
rectangle that represents all that they have done in that
cold month. You know that it is never anything
to look forward to; you pass it on as quickly
as you can, like a shame the bank your scapegoat
accepts. That paper gestates, and gives birth to
more paper that you can store, carry and wave around,
to pick out boxes upon boxes of nothing that
resembles food, in the chilled section of your local
NTUC Fairprice.
        What were your expectations
for this work? Sometimes you seek out the hidden
green patches, like Mount Emily and Labrador Park,
to colonise a bench and try not to regulate
the fluid and mild electricity of the morning air.
You remember the article you had read, somewhere,
on a breezier day: how college students at Dartmouth,
where BASIC was invented and terminals abound,
sometimes went out of campus to their own organic farm
to tend lettuce and red cabbage and sweet peas.

You can almost see the salad in the cafeteria,
topped off by red wine vinaigrette. There are streaks
of colour, like rose essence on lemongrass, a carpet fair
in a souk, colour blindness tests. Basil jelly on almond
cream. Beethoven on speed. Velvet on sponge.
Here you lay claim to what should have been yours,
unsheltered in a town you negotiate through enough taxi-rides
to suggest that the conduct of your reassignments
isn't yours; but for a moment you can put behind you
your demiurgical negation, in a space of your own creation,
somewhere in between the vacant pocket-money and
the rich gold piercing your eyelids in a throb of blood,
which in your living room would be coming in
through the windows, and the slits of blinds.

THE HAPPINESS OF MEANING IN THE NEW ECONOMY

So each morning you stop by the Botero bird, facing the bumboats
chugging on the bumps, breathing river stink in lieu of sea breeze
and taking up your load. It's been like this since you gave in,
trading stress for unhappiness, citing the airy economy and how
the Morgan Stanleys and McKinseys of this world have stopped
                                                recruiting,
making the head go where the heart would not be seen dead,
and turning, each evening, to the malt and smoke and bitter sweat
of the upturned barrels, almost authentically beer-soaked wood floor
and pooled lampgold of the cavern that is Muddy Murphy's.

There you remember the feline eyes of the redhead whose breasts you
almost put your nose into while she praised her baby-oil push-up bra,
for you would shag her in an instant, drunk or not so drunk,
even as you work to lust for a woman you talked into bed, willing
to love her with pay. She will be another scenic distraction
in the dust-smudge of the right wing mirror, beside the traffic
of your incoherence. You have to knock yourself awake, to
gather up the worth to open the window and let the evening out,
though it's already morning, for whatever that means.

Every word traded in waste that day is in another view an investment,
burning up the ecological semiotics of the polyester world,
promising fists raining down will pull the catgut so it yowls
in the hollow of violins. You die a little every time
you put aside your hoard. You long, you thirst, you want to want first
that burst of meaningfulness so nearly like a desert-drink of joy.
You need to feed your wants into the future's astronomical maw.
In such a richness there will always be your case.
You have to sculpt your face. Choose your drug. Ring your broker.

HR IN THE TIME OF RECESSION

Screening candidates for employment is an odd task.
There're stacks and stacks of CVs to go through,
and each of them is a life. Most don't stack up,
most hope to be given a chance, though some
are so far out in left field they're in the stands.
What does one do with a multi-lingual Chinese
nuclear scientist asking nine hundred US dollars
for an intermediate-level marketing position?
Or the local graduate who says her application
to our company is no accident, but "an astute choice",
because we are "well-known for our training" and
"have a good reputation regionally", which would have
flattered us were we not a 4-month-old 6-man startup.
After a while it becomes voyeuristic. You see the fear
in their reduced asking salaries, mutter at their mistakes,
curse at those who miss the requirements by a Bubka vault,
smile at evidence of determined, continued self-improvement.
You peer into their mugshots as though their eyes might meet yours,
wondering what they would have been like if you had met them,
even as you toss their CVs into piles; most of all, though the odds
are against you, you wish you could give them hope, a better life,
the opportunity to prove themselves, to pull themselves
from the swamp of dreary afternoons sat writing cover letters,
until you see, within a celibate and private flash,
the imperfectly perfect patterns of Bridget Riley:
those irresistible and tantric paintings, those
perfect-imperfect lines that if you stare at too long
will purple out real things.

PRINTING MONEY

As my dad used to say whenever he
thought we were spending all his thrift,
do you think I print money? I didn't really
know at that time whether to take him seriously.
I mean, I was eight, maybe nine. My concept of
money extended to what I got for wanton mee
at school recess only, and everything else I
asked for knowing who would give it to me
but not what this person would do to give it.
One December, shopping at Isetan, he pretended
to refuse to buy me a die-cast Millennium Falcon,
and when I returned to that special aisle and shelf
in the toy department the last one was gone,
the absent shrine of a forgetful grief. My dad
unwrapped it, under the tree, for a boy who
still believed Santa Claus came down the chimney,
even though we had no chimney. Dad believed
in the deserts of hard work, years and years
with the same employer, saving money by
fixing the blinds and electrical extensions himself.
Never quite recovered when his firm let him go,
three years before retirement age. Now that I've aged
also, and the difference between a good year
and a bad year is a greenback hedge, I know.
My dad doesn't print money, but someone out there
does. It all revolves on being on the right side
of that ocean-equation, whether you're holding Treasuries
and knowing how to deploy the funds you haven't got.
Someone's got to lose, just as somewhere in the world
the stratonimbus plan a margin-call, and elsewhere
beneath molten sky unwearied Namibians speak again
of the season of dry water, stretching endlessly
before them, shimmering like silver, one remove
from the hardtack stop-loss of the ground,
that forgiving, unnourished, ageless ground.

OIL

I'm standing at the pumps, gunning Premium 98
into my tank and looking at the convenience store
bright as a robbery target, when it occurs to me
we pass a million dead bodies through our engines
every day: plankton, coelacanth and other bottom-dwellers,
pterodactyl. Which gives me food for thought:
when we set off our own catastrophe,
exchanging nuclear bombs like Christmas cards
or setting smallpox loose upon the world again,
will the next civilizations use us for fuel?
It's better than going to waste in a cemetery,
though why we haven't installed generators
in our crematoria is beyond me, possibly
beyond even a politician's oily tongue.
I would want to burn in a poet's car,
when he's starting it up in his garage, where the
recursive whiff of combusted fuel will throng
his nostrils, oiling his mind to think:
that could be me. He'd shift to first gear,
press down the accelerator, slide out of his driveway
into an avenue where the trees are throwing *feuilles mortes*
to the wind, so they might float, like uncontained ashes,
into a dreamless out of sight.

PAPER LANTERNS

Escaping fumes of frying oil at Hong Lim food centre,
we crossed the connector to the next block, whose corridors
of beauty parlours and traditional Chinese medicine clinics
lead to the overhead bridge channeling us back
to cubicles anchored in the sky, but their practical promise
vanished while growing larger all the time as my colleague
eddied in the human stream, to gaze upon a row of lanterns
suspended from an aluminium trellis. It was Mid-Autumn,
and our estates were inundated with children bearing light.
I tried to stay out of the way, but as soon as I saw him
fingering the battery-operated inflatable plastic Ultraman
without looking at it I knew he had sent his heart
over to where the paper lanterns hung. I remembered
how my dad would unpack the flat layers of colour,
bend the wires in place, insert the candleholder
and the candle, carefully lower a match into the belly
of the fish or butterfly and then hand the rod to me,
but then flamed up more intensely in me the memory
of playing cops-and-robbers, and, while looking out
for the other kids, neglecting how my lantern was resting
only to turn and see the string low in the hollow
of my blue rabbit, the orange clambering up the string
and eating at the paper. Whether I howled in grief
or stood stupidly watching loss taking shape
is beside the point, though its transient obduracy
has burnt itself into my register of reasons to feel cold
on tropical nights. Even if this could have been avoided
it would not have changed the flow of our fallibility,
the tragedy of learning when it has become too late,
for to feel like nothing before or since is progress
that cannot be wrapped in plastic or flicked like a switch:
I didn't know then that the blue rabbit was just a thing,
not a destination or crystallised permanence,
but a means to an end, a controlled trial by fire,

a vaccine by which to make light the loss yet to come,
which will come not with thunder and lightning
or fire and brimstone, but with the backdrop of night,
the soak of the full moon, the gentle weeping of stars.

CROW-SHOOTERS

I was nestled in a hammock on the balcony,
soaking in a siesta in the post-rain afternoon,
when the noise-shocks erupted, sudden blasts
like localised thunder, cracks of a celestial whip.
I recognised them from army days, whipped off
my hammock and caught sight of flights of birds
flapping frantically clear of the treeline,
into the backdrop of clouds, then, on the lane
to the left, the men, wearing polo tee-shirts
encased in beige vests and holding long rifles.
One wore sunglasses atop his cap, another had
split his barrel from his stock and was inserting
another round. Crow-shooters. Sunglasses
took out a rubber glove and snapped it on while
crossing to the grassy bank to bag his earnings.
I recalled how, walking home donkeyed with bags
from the supermarket, I had cast a doubtful eye on
the crows, foot-long sentinels in robes glossy and
black as ink on their high perch of streetlights,
not really knowing what I was watching out for.
Not knowing if anything could ever shake
that robber-baron assurance. And here, now,
was the cavalry, the crow-shooters, laying the sins
I couldn't imagine on this murder of scared crows,
and, in that same fluid alignment of the rifle sights,
burdening me with the undoubting pre-emption
of my unkind nation, in whose name only will I be
able to walk up the lane with lowered head.

MIRRORS

If breaking a mirror brings seven years of bad luck,
what happens if I don't break a mirror? I ask
because last night while shuffling the decks
on my unruly desk I knocked over a fold-out mirror,
but caught it before it plunged the yard to the ground.
It's not the fall that breaks things, of course, but
perhaps with balance sheets on my mind I wondered
if that meant I was due seven years of good luck;
if I didn't have liability, surely I had equity?
Or did it just mean I was quits? On the other hand,
if my left one had not been quick enough to jam-press
the mirror to the desk edge, how would I have known
which misfortunes would have had to be due to the mirror's
unsettled spirits? Would I look back and thank my stars
for a catch that saved a sprained wrist becoming
a broken arm? Or, had the silvered glass ushered
my explosive entry into another life-stream, could it have
refinanced its mortgage, shattering a son in the sixth year?
I think of looking into rearview mirrors and trying
to remember its objects are closer than they appear,
though it seems my objects are never close at hand
whether I pass them or not, and if that is what
a mirror does, I cannot tell where ifs become whens,
what luck takes which direction, and whether
what appears to be has already come, and gone.

PUNCTURE

It was on the road to Ipoh that I copped a flat tire,
and the swarthy Indian who almost instantly drew up
to offer a ride to a petrol kiosk in his Nissan pick-up
pricked my pride, so I had to fix it myself.
I detached the panniers, flipped the Shimano over
on the damp sandy shoulder, loosened the brake wires,
unlocked the wheel, fished out the bike levers,
prised the tire from the rim and slid the inner tube out.
I was on the outskirts of a village, and goodness knows
how minor miracles happen but a Malay gardener
in a backyard fifty metres down lent me a bucket
and enough water in it to loop the inner tube through,
track down a trail of champagne bubbles and find
the pinprick. When the inner tube dried, I squeezed on resin,
then added a patch. I fitted the half-inflated tube into the tire,
rolled the lip of the tire round the rim, then pumped it up
with a hand-pump, reattached the wheel and fixed the brakes.
Even if it took forty-five minutes and I only reached Ipoh
after sun-down, no one would have known I'd had a puncture.
But I did. It was never the same as before. I watched my tire
with new anxiety. Scowled at the road. Waited for a blow-out.

BRUT

And what's so unreal about the endless pouring of champagne?
To hear the gentle kiss of a cork sliding loose and the mousse sighing
its giving openness, to see the beads rising in rapid formation
out of nothing, like a string of pearls, finally to feel them frothing
on your tongue with a tart taste balanced by the douceur of dosage,
brings itself forth self-assured of nothing quite so real, so lightly,
as itself; for champagne has not the sombre density of a Chambertin,
it is nothing quite so grounded or authoritative, nothing quite
so deep, but if you realise that the beads you run over your tongue
are the stored exhalation of dead yeast, how can you not find
in its being both the palliative and the excitement of your pain
the contest of contrary forces that drives towards an absolute,
which is realness? It is with that knowledge that you can face
the unreal: who will archive the breath that you waste now,
sighing for your beloved? She who is all divine nimbus
you cannot touch, however drawn like a vapour to her,
and if that is where champagne leads you it is not so much
that its secondary fermentations are outside of its bottle
but that its approach through the agency of the real is diabolical
and in that sense may be as unreal as sex, or roulette tables,
and therefore what is truly inescapable about the whole ritual
of popping mushroom corks and exercising the real in the gentle
tuning-fork hum of Riedel glasses that have kissed and passed
is how you want to do it, over and over and over again.

POSTDATE

Interpreting a date is an impossible task. So let's see...
You found occasion to touch me a couple of times,
which was good. We had an extended conversation
about films, it was light and funny, which was good.
I had an awful line about walking in the metro station,
which was bad. You didn't compliment me, but I
squeezed in a compliment I don't know if you heard,
which was like catching a taxi only to not have change
for the fare. You proposed dessert after the film,
which was earning a replay bonus in a game of pinball.
I didn't mention any other women but you asked me
to translate a flirty SMS, and I'm not sure why you did that
but it was like having the opening for insider trading
knowing full well what the risks were. Were you curious?
I think so, but I was certainly curious about you,
which was showing my hand in poker with the calm
of not being able to influence yours. Occasionally
we waded through such ambient noise you misheard me,
which was spilling Haut-Brion rouge on a white silk shirt
with most of the evening still to go. All these moments
come to a collage that is clearer and still unknown,
just as all the maps of the world can never prepare you
for the instant you crest the plateau and the evening sun
bursts the shackles of foliage to warm the valley
opening up before you like cupped palms, collecting gold.

POST MORTEM

When I get to heaven I will ask God
to point out to me all the things I've done
wrong in my life. He'd start with the sins,
of course, rebuking me for stealing the coins
off the dresser, for not helping my neighbour
debug his computer when I had the time,
and maybe even for watching American Idol.
I'd sit through this all, feeling worse
and worse about myself, but nonetheless
patiently, only because I want to know
where missteps had cost me a better life.
He'd sigh, maybe shrug, and then tell me.
If I had studied economics instead of
anthropology. If I had not taken a gap year.
"You should have asked Christina out," he'd say.
"I'd set up everything perfectly in place for you.
How much more clear did you need the clues?"
And then he'd come to you. "What did I do
wrong there?" I'd ask. "Things were going fine,
and then..." He'd pause, and ponder, and pace
around the hall, and finally he'd say: "You've
got me there. That's just the way she is."
And the unexplained mystery of my earthly life
will become a legend spreading like a virus
through the firmament, adding to unhatched
typhoons and, every now and then, sparking off
a shooting star spearing through the blackness.

BLACK

The day I gulped black coffee from the café round the corner
and spat out a boiled flying ant was the day coffee became
irredeemably bitter. What had been not so much
black gold as a periodic refill of a fueltank of consciousness
came to taste of wormwood and lacquer, and that
undiminishable moment when paracetamol gets stuck
in the back of one's throat. But it wasn't till much later
that I realised it was also the day you left to start a new life
in Switzerland, and if we who gathered at the airport
to wave you through the departure gates tried to pretend
ours was only a temporary parting we also knew there were ways
in which distance could enforce its own gravitational physics.
As you were packing and filling in insurance forms I had tried
to map out for you the undulation of my emotional geographies,
but couldn't, and you had to lean over and hold me together.
I realised: I have so much to say and nothing to say,
and this implied inability to build structures out of, or around,
my raw stories is like the refusal of a wound to heal. I wanted to write
a song for the unknown and unknowable looking glass you had
brought to me, but it is possible to want something too much.
When I was younger and we lived where refugee flying ants
sought amnesty from the late March rains, my mother had
dealt with them by placing a large white porcelain bowl of water
underneath a lamp, and the ants, hypnotised by the wrong light,
would plunge headfirst in, only to drown. I'm not going to drown –
this much I promise you – but if all there is to look forward to
is a future fractioned out by the blackest, bitterest liquid,
which I sustain even as it sustains me, how the other blackness,
the daily oblivion remembering its blood-tie to *oublier*,
becomes a patch of yellow grass on the other side,
that far and nebulously other side, somewhere round the corner.

SELLING SHORT

An advertisement for a condominium in the business district reads:
"Feel the life around the corner." The reflex response:
life should be right here, right now. It reminds me
of the advert for a brand of mattress promising truly
dreamless sleep, not awake to the possibility that
if dreams make our caffeinated hours worthwhile
the encrypted missives they bring us at night
craft magic to drive us to find truth in illusions,
and remake our worlds with the conviction of copy.
In this way we learn that maybe is its own democracy;
change is the only constant, except from a vending machine;
memory is a keen photographer, but uses black and white;
imperfection has its charm, but it doesn't always work.
What does work is that they help us to feel
we've got a handle on underrated complexities,
and we can wake up each morning certain that this is life
as we have wanted to live it. If we simmer our dreams
enough, they reduce to the consistency of faith,
but if we buy the promises of advertisements,
what dreams may come are the platitudes of the every other,
but, either road, pouncing like a wolf out of the night
is the dream of missing a step or tripping over a stick,
triggered by a dip in blood pressure or a change in the tides
in the middle ear, and we wake with a jolt, denied
the continuation of story, which way the leaves fall.

PEELING A CLEMENTINE

Falling into a rock-cave, your fingernail
pierces past the soft skin to a core of hollow,
then you rip the waxen orange away like wallpaper.
Meanwhile the people on the train hate you,
as though you'd set off a car alarm in a quiet street.
Their alarms are telling them it's time, time, time for lunch,
if only they weren't somewhere between Durham and Newcastle.
If only you had been more patient. You remember the stories
of Japanese sushi apprentices having to slave two years
before receiving the master's permission to touch a knife,
and even then, their first year is spent carving the *baren*,
the plastic grass that separates the wasabi from the *nigiri*.
You separate the fistful from the peel and split the heart in half.
Your palm is warm with anticipation and immediacy. It feels
like that morning you woke early and watched from a hot spring
the sun rising between the trees in Akita Prefecture.
She was in bed, unmoving, with her lips slightly apart.
You part your lips slightly to receive a segment.
It's sweet but refreshing only for its acid.

HUNGRY GHOST MONTH

In Hungry Ghost month, the Chinese refuse to buy property,
because the Gates of Hell are flung open and the spirits swarm
out of the underworld for their much-needed annual vacation,
pirouetting through our world and staining everything they touch
with a residue of bad luck. It's their kind of bad luck that made
Third Uncle lose his job and Fourth Aunt ram her Renault
into the back of a Fedex van, leaving her with concussion and
scores of executives wondering what mischief had waylaid
their express-delivery documents, none of them caveats.
Most hatefully, half my extended family blamed the ghosts
for leading my cousin over the edge, and wouldn't believe me
when I said the root cause of his suicide was, clearly, love.
Even as a kid I thought these visitors should have been called
Wicked Ghosts, not Hungry Ghosts, if they were truly at fault;
but I wasn't sure then that one couldn't take all that adults said
at face value, and in any case was willing to go along with it
for steamed chicken after the famished ancestors had eaten.
Now, it doesn't bother me to scamper to the kitchen in the dark
for a midnight egg sandwich. It doesn't seem likely mere halogen
would help me see them more clearly, because I don't believe
in them, just as the Incas did not see the Spanish ships drop
anchor because nothing so outlandishly fantastical could exist,
and though one should always take the necessary precautions
whether skydiving or crossing the road, all the same I like to think
that even if I don't believe in them, they still believe in us.

SNAKE WINE

Not until my second last morning did I break
beyond Pasteur Street to Ben Thanh market,
whose exterior did not hint at the dimensions
of its accepting harvests, and the way I got there
was by braving the Saigon traffic on a pillion seat,
darting in between and around swarms of scooters
and taxis trying to make it through the same junctions
all together, while the wind of my helpless movement
blew the scent of the woman in front of me,
with tickling wisps of her hair, at me; but this is not
about her, or how she would start with lightly humoured
petulance whenever I strode into her room. Rather,
after twenty minutes of flicking our fingers through
handmade chopsticks with accompanying ivory rests
and miniature dolls selling the fantasy of a Vietnam
subtly curved in *áo dài*, we came across rows and rows
of violin-case-shaped bottles filled with yellow wine
and a baby king cobra each, glassy-eyed, stiff-tongued,
fangs visible as with intent, its patterned grey hood
enriched by a deep orange dot of Chinese wolfsberry.
I wondered if one could be an appropriate gift for you;
you hatched in the Year of the Snake, and you had the bite
of a woman. We assume these coils are dead,
but I remembered the news report on the Thai bachelor
who had uncorked a bottle only for the cobra
to spring out from organic hibernation to bury its fangs
deep into his knuckles, and I thought that you would
surely never taste the liquor if I told you that story,
which would mean it could rest on your bedside ledge
as a permanently dreamcatching souvenir of me.

SHIRT MAINTENANCE IN THE TROPICS

In the tropics it's not the cuffs nor the buttons
that wear out first, it's the collar. Sweat stains,
from your neck being on the line too often,
discolour the fabric's horizon. You can wash it out
with Persil, but cotton dyes never stay fast,
whatever the label tells you, and the noonday blaze
helps to lighten the vibrancy of what holds
your silk tie in place. In Singapore, if I were
sweating on a risky position, I could buy security
with a zero-cost option collar, but in Vietnam
to be wearing Alain Figaret and rimless glasses
on Dong Khoi Street could be all the risk
you could stomach, like the mixed plate of limp
mint and basil and coriander that accompanies
each bowl of phở. Last week, as I awaited
the opening to hopskotch across to Mac Thi Buoi
someone all but collared me. I spun around,
flung my fists out, almost caught him on the chin
as he pitched me, "Girl, you want, many pretty girl,"
and as we eyed each other we didn't know who
was more surprised. I thought, no thanks,
I'll keep my shirt on. I should have cuffed him
but I wear my heart on my sleeve, and that's why
I might lose my shirt and it scares the pants off me.

THE INTERNMENT OF SNAILS

It was all reasonable to begin with. A colleague
kept an aquarium in the office. Aswirl with plecos,
shimmery cyan neon tetra and transparent catfish,
it took him away from intensely interlinked spreadsheets
every other hour, and improved the *feng shui* at his desk
to boot. One day, he added a black log into the aquarium,
but there must have been a couple of stowaway snails
cached in a cranny, for within a week we found a battery
of spiral shells creeping up the walls, or perched
on the *elodea densa*. No one thought more of them,
not even when they multiplied, until we figured that
the eggs the corys were laying on the aquarium walls
were being hoovered up by the snails. At once we set about
fishing them out – air-rifle pellets and pebbles,
black conicals and baby translucent spirals –
and resettling them into a new home, a smaller tank
that we airlifted the log into and filled with water.
Only, every few hours we would see more renegades
creeping up the aquarium walls. We caught them too,
and those that came after. At first we watched the snails
in their new enclosure with some fascination;
some glided upside-down from the surface of the water
while others ran races around the walls or hid
in the java moss we had added to the snail camp.
Occasionally we threw in a pinch of fish flakes.
Yet it seemed that for every gastropod we captured
another sprang up from unknown aquarium depths.
Meanwhile the second tank grew concentrated with snails.
Hundreds studded the log; some feelered their way
through layered droppings submerged in murky water.
Nobody wanted to clean the tank. We didn't know how
to change a water chock-full of rebellious molluscs,
couldn't see how many tiny deaths there were
in that rout of snails, didn't know what to do with them.

Someone suggested salt, or introducing a loach,
for whom the escargatoire would be a buffet. My colleague
said he would flush the lot of them down the toilet.
We dawdled till they died, of overcrowding and their own
pollution, and over the weekend the tank disappeared,
only to reappear on acidic nights, when silvery trails
lead where whatever we can reasonably do catches us
unaware how efficient we can be, which is, we freely say,
in light of what we want to achieve, a small price to pay.

DURIANS

During my last reservist stint, in Ama Keng,
that unmistakable waft: like garbage and onions
and liquid petroleum gas all mixed in one. We jerked
our helmeted heads upward, and saw the spiky bombs.
Durians. Two soldiers waded into the lallang and long
spiky-grassed undergrowth, sweeping for fallen fruit.
I remembered what my dad once told me,
that durian trees knew when you were underneath
and would not let their deadly payload drop.
They were smarter than we thought; those things could
kill. For when they had spent the years
building up to seed, they did not want to waste
their chance by murdering their postmen.
It spoke husks about why we were there,
stuck in sweatstink and number four fatigues,
when a drive by Dempsey Road could have reaped
D24 fruit from Selangor. I guess we take
what we can get. All the same, I couldn't help
thinking of the Filipino legend, in which a hermit
made a fruit to help a king win over a princess,
then cursed it when the king neglected to invite him
to the wedding feast; and we've been eating it ever since.

AUBERGINES

The purest expression of your love was in your cooking aubergines.
You called them brinjals, after the Indian fashion, sometimes eggplants.
You hated the bitterness you were more sensitive to than I was,
you thought a violet-black face could only bring gall.
In Sanskrit it was vatin-gana, the plant that cured the wind.
Cooked incorrectly, it could be bitter, odd-textured, herald of wind.
You made sure my aubergines were perfect. You didn't panic
when the spongelike flesh drank hissing sunflower oil.
The Arabs knew it as al-badinjan. In Marrakesh,
I had aubergines roasted over a charcoal fire, lightly salted.
You stuck to fried fish, washing it down with sweet mint tea.
We crossed the Straits of Gibraltar, where the fruit became alberengena
and then aubergine. We once dined at Aubergine, in London,
before Gordon Ramsay moved to the Royal Hospital Road,
where he promptly installed a carpet darker than royal purple.
To the east, badinjan became melongena, melanzana, mela insana.
I was your mad apple. The Portuguese called it bringella,
and when they landed in Goa their guns brought a word
puréed through innumerable monsoons in the Andaman Sea to you.
In the West Indies, it became, differently, the brown-jolly.
Once the oil hit a fiercely crackling heat, the aubergine's brave
structure collapsed and much of the oil was re-released.
We lease our spirits from our languages. All these names for the
                                                    same fruit:
the same bulbous expression of energy, pushed through roots
and leaves and stems to still and concentrate as goodness and evil,
shiny and soft. I call them aubergines. You call them brinjals.

LADY'S FINGER

At dinner with friends, our hostess outdid herself
with an exceptional tiramisu: three days' jogging worth
of mascarpone and brandy, and coffee-soaked
ladyfinger, which you oohed over, so I mentioned
how my well-thumbed Concise Oxford didn't agree
with the Shorter in suggesting that lady's finger
was either sponge finger or a small flowering plant
that blooms in Europe between April and September,
while ladies' fingers meant *abelmoschus esculentus*,
also known as okra, or gumbo, or, in my dictionary,
ugh. You said that language as well as vegetables
was supposed to be organic, and the later Shorter,
interlacing all the possible fingers as if in prayer,
could have been conveniently solving a problem.
What if we eat just one of them? I asked you.
It was difficult to conceive of ladies' finger. Anyway,
I added, your fingers would not feed anybody,
meaning I had admired how slender yours were,
but you thought, or pretended to think, I'd twigged
you couldn't cook. Not that it mattered; that you
did the washing-up despite a cut on your finger
told me more than the clearest words you could pick,
and that you could pick me up with a few thoughtful
words when I was tired nevertheless whitewashed
how much uncertainty of words had come between us
with the deliberate indecision of indeterminacy
we held in common without sharing. But if we had
to trade aporia for our lexical truths, our fiction
was less strange than fact, yet our belief made it
more or less than what it was: I had to hand it to you,
I couldn't put my finger on it. It had become the way
coffee and brandy and mascarpone all blended
into one, on the softened structure of the ladyfinger.

RUBESCO VIGNA MONTICCHIO

It seems just like an illusion now,
projected on the sheen of my glass of wine,
how you had just emerged from the Museo Vaticano
and I'd been round the block with two gelati,
only to find, when we reached an ATM,
that we had drawn down my account
and thus had only 17.000 lire
to last another week.
After we cabled money urgently,
we crossed the Tiber, I window-shopped for wine
and we bought bread and cheese for dinner,
sat like penurious artists in Piazza di Navona.
All this comes back to me now as I sip
my glass of 1990 Rubesco Vigna Monticchio,
which I bought, of course, the next time
we were in Rome. I've been to Rome
six times, I think, and was last there
with you. You threw my coin into the Trevi.
I don't believe it lies there still.

PHOTOGRAPHY IN THE AGE OF DIGITAL

The third time I went to Bangkok I didn't
even bring my camera, which is not
to say that I knew the place so well
nor that it had suddenly lost
what gave it colour, but that I was no longer
in the same need of scrapbook memories.
I went to my Bangkok tailor by a route I knew
by walking, and the way he fussed over me
brought me back to being a schoolboy
in a camera shop in Peninsula Plaza,
where the salesman who looked after me
either thought of his own son or was glad
just to have someone other than tourists
to speak to, for he sold me my first Nikon
for less than what he got from a Korean walk-in
a few weeks later, when I dropped by.
Or else he guessed I would make good use of it,
would come back for telephoto and macro lenses -
different ways of seeing the object
I was training my eye on - or he already knew
what it was like to have shot one's life in pieces,
and to be a piece of someone else's life,
however like an impression in shot silk,
is not to be missed, whatever the lighting
and the film speed, just as freezing things
on silver halides is less important than
what it says to have tried, for repeated trials
tell the photographer all he needs to know
about who he has been and where he is,
and other such cheaply purchased knowledge.

TRAJECTORIES

To the side of the game on the big screen –
Saturday night, FA Cup fifth round – come
a couple of teenagers, the taller one maybe
sitting for his IB and the other still shedding
baby fat. They put coins in the slot and slide it
to set off the sound of phenolic resin rolling
down the drains. There is the satisfying clack
of the balls racked right, and then the smack
and clatter of the break. Over the clipped notes
of Martin Tyler they're shooting the balls,
one with a little draw, the other with a little luck.
Around them the aroma of English ale
and the martingale of pub chatter have carved
a space to be ignored in, but as the boys
bend over the baize to take shots one-third full
to the far pocket I try the other choices
they could have not surrendered to conjecture.
Whether the white would have wound up
back in the kitchen for the nine is at the unlocatable
juncture of eyesight and bicep and the precise
wearing of the playing surface, and I should know
but if they ask I shall shrug and sip my pint,
and when I place my glass back on its mat
right on cue the girl I've been waiting for will arrive
and pull me by my fingers out of the chair
as though to tango, and I in her embrace will
look up and spot an enormous *lyssa zampa*
resting on a rafter, the Milky Way running down
each black wing like a trajectory or the end in sight.

RIESLING

There's nothing finer for the summer
than a glass of Mosel Riesling, its light green
colour dancing with so much breaking sunlight
it scatters a shadow play all over the straw mat.
Don't be so surprised. I've always pretended
not to like Riesling, which can be true
when I sip a particularly aggressive one
smelling as though it has just been crushed out
from underneath the chassis of your VW,
but when it tastes of lemonade and peaches,
and the alternative is Pimms, forgive me
for not being quite what you had expected.
If it's surprise that makes good wine great,
let us not always be able to read each other
like summer bestsellers to be remaindered
by the time we share a glass of – I don't know –
Sauvignon Blanc the next hot Oxford summer.
Last summer, I didn't expect you'd feed the ducks
bread dipped in wine; less still that they
would take the bread and wash it in the river
before gulping down their sodden pickings.
You hadn't expected we'd find our restless spirits
growing in communion. But if we now want
to eat our cake and have it, and in so trying
embed sorrow, should it bring you to blink
that I now pull the cork on a thin green bottle
and produce, as if by an undeserved magic,
two impractically tall, tulip-shaped glasses?

TIONG BAHRU

However you may have intended it to be
a continuity from the ease of student life,
you knew that Jules had only conceded
when her arguments skipped banging tables
to knocking over chairs, and Jack's uncaring
fluidity, with which he picked up chicks in Rouge,
drew a yes without a thought from him, and I,
well, I wasn't there to make up the number.
That the Tiong Bahru flat was your granny's
and she in a home for senile dementia meant
we didn't have to meet rent, but to feed four
fresh mouths with no jobs and babyskin hopes
was enough to uncover unknown deaths in us.
We swallowed our prides in scrounging
used stock bones from the corner *zi char* stall
to top plain white rice with a dash of soy sauce.
Jack picked cigarette butts off the pavements
to roll slim blends we would pass around,
which even I could not resist. Evenings
we breathed out at the door, with the swishing
of the sweeps of cleaners scratching our ears
lightly. Dusk was hazily sad. I knew I could
go back, but if I'd imagined common suffering
would tear up the fabric that marked bedless space
and entitled no one to secret feelings then
I hadn't grasped how accentuated lonelinesses
could build to selfishness like an electric current
about to blow a fuse, and how, when you
found a job and moved out, it was as though
by an unnecessary gesture you were setting down
how sure you were what we had was not ours
to claim. I know now that I can think back
without hopelessly contained rage that you
were in your own confidence correct, that

we had come together in happy convenience,
and finally that some places and circumstances
don't belong to us now, maybe never did.

LOVE WHERE LOVE IS KNOWN

Every lover is a quisling.
Whether love buds or its new crimson edge is
torn off by impatience, you do not know how much
it animates you. You fall into the comfortable clothes
of a leading part. You retreat into the unsaid.
What you do not say turns your stomach in being less than fact.
You send the plumbline after how much depth there is
between new lovers, when touch flows into surfaces
and planes, when our feel of warmth becomes our invisible
blanket. Love blossoms after the conquest of self-pity.
You strain after the movements. When your bodied locks
become as much as all there is between you, your thigh
in between your lover's, inextricable as coral on the seabed,
you do not speak because of what that must sell, or purchase.
You only stop your mouths with a kiss. You do not know when
the final movement of the piece and the final locking of mouths
will be. And if you have watched the curtain fall, you would be
more guarded about whom you could extend your inside to
than ever before. Of course, there is always a cluttered background,
talkshow-type stuff about how you were brought up, but
in such a tableau how distant you can make yourself,
like a door ajar, as though someone were peeking out,
never daring to open the iron gate, never daring to step out
into a fermenting warmth, as the sun ascends and chases the chill
of another neutral morning away, becomes a virtue where you must
make the world your own, claiming its weakest, most vulnerable parts.

The bedclothes are twisted. You climb out of bed against the sun,
furl a dressing gown, slouch into the kitchen where you smack an egg
against the side of a saucepan sizzling with canola oil, and
put the kettle to a race against the egg. Why choose? you ask.
Why not continually savour the first flush of love like the first high
of a first cup of coffee, and not be so inured you drink it for the taste,
or for the form? If you take hold of your needs and your under-hate,
you might just be able to chisel out the form of your love
and test the adage that you say but have not connected with,
that love is what we make of it.

ACKNOWLEDGEMENTS

Ars Interpres (Sweden) for 'The Internment of Snails'

Asheville Poetry Review (USA) for 'Postdate'

Atlanta Review (USA) for 'HR in the time of recession'

Blackmail Press (New Zealand) for 'Home Improvement'

Cider Press Review (USA) for 'The Happiness of Meaning in the New Economy'

Language for a New Century: Contemporary Poetry from the Middle East, Asia, and Beyond (USA) for 'Crow-Shooters'

Dream Catcher (UK) for 'Peeling A Clementine'

Fabric Poems (UK) for 'Rubesco Vigna Monticchio'

In Our Own Words (USA) for reprinting 'The Happiness of Meaning in the New Economy'

Lamport Court (UK) for 'Worth Remembering'

London Review of Books (UK) for 'Durians'

Madelaine (UK) for 'Riesling'

Mascara (Australia) for 'Snake Wine'

91st Meridian (USA) for reprinting 'Oil'

Over There: Poems from Singapore and Australia (Singapore) for 'Paper Lanterns' and 'Selling Short', and for reprinting 'Aubergines', 'Oil', and 'Printing Money'

papertiger (Australia) for 'Oil'

Poetry Salzburg Review (Austria) for 'Aubergines'

Softblow (Singapore) for 'Printing Money'

Toh Hsien Min is the author of *Iambus* and *The Enclosure of Love*. He is also the founding editor of the *Quarterly Literary Review Singapore*, a former president of the Oxford University Poetry Society and a recipient of the 1996 Shell-National Arts Council Scholarship for the Arts.

Hsien Min works in the financial services industry, where he holds CFA and FRM certifications.